1

James Earl Carter, Jr

(Jimmy Carter)

Hail to the Chief Series

Keith Pruitt

Words of Wisdom

2025

In Memory of

President Jimmy Carter

Introduction

When President Jimmy Carter turned 100 years old on October 1, 2024, many knew his days were few. He had already been in hospice care for over a year, and the frailness was obvious when the family released footage of the backyard celebration. His beloved Rosalynn had passed away on November 19, 2023. The Carters had celebrated their 77th wedding anniversary having married in 1946. Theirs was the longest Presidential marriage in history. He struggled in the last several months, but the nation took heart when the family released a statement from the former President in October that he wanted to live long enough to vote for Kamala Harris for President. And he did. But less than a week after Christmas, as the author was setting in a restaurant on a Sunday afternoon, a push notification announced the passing of the 29th President. And a nation mourned.

Jimmy Carter was a different kind of politician. His downhome, small town roots had shaped him into a man who loved God, loved his family, and loved his country. In another century, Jimmy Carter would have been the appropriate subject of a Horatio Alger story, much like James Garfield. Plains, Georgia boasts about 700 persons. It's close to Americus, and most folks haven't heard of it either. But the characters of the Carter story were indeed characters. Jimmy's parents, James Earl Carter, Sr. and Mrs. Lillian were solid, hard-working, down-to-earth kind of people. Earl was a successful farmer with a bent toward progressivism. He'd even figured out a way of having water pumped to the house using a water tower run by wind energy. Funny thing is, it is still working today. Mr. Carter was most successful as a peanut farmer. He also ran the general store in town. About a year after he was elected to the state legislature, he died.

Ms. Lillian was a kindhearted, humble woman who believed in education and service. She was a registered nurse, thus the reason that her son, Jimmy, was born in a hospital. James was a great deal like his mother. Even in her advanced years, Lillian Carter joined the Peace Corp. Then there was brother Billy, the rough talking, beer loving brother who owned a gas station right next to the police station. Ruth Carter became an evangelist, and his sister Gloria was a noted motorcycle enthusiast. Ruth had been Rosalynn's best friend.

The family had lived out of town a piece in a community mostly populated by blacks. Carter learned to respect racial differences at a very early age even in a state that maintained segregation as the rule. Much of the character development resulted from this early childhood. Through the depression and war, the family kept at their task. Their spiritual life centered around bible reading, prayer, Sunday School and worship at the Plains Baptist Church. And it was against this backdrop, that Jimmy Carter came to prominence.

Come along on our journey as we honor the wonderful life of Jimmy Carter. 100 years of life. He was the servant of people. And when the end came, a nation came together to say, "Thank You."

President Jimmy Carter at the LBJ Presidential Library, 2014, Courtesy the Carter Center

James Earl Carter, Jr.

Born: October 1, 1924 in Plains, Georgia
Died: December 29, 2024 in Plains, Georgia
Parents: James Earl Carter, Sr. and Bessie Lillian Gordy
Spouse: Roselyn Smith
Occupation: Naval officer, Georgia State Senator, Governor of Georgia, 39th President of the United States, Founded the Carter Center, Sunday School Teacher
Religion: Southern Baptist
Political Party: Democrat
Vice President: Walter Mondale
President Carter became the first former President to receive the Noble Peace Prize, 2002, Jimmy Carter was also the first President born in a hospital. He was the longest-lived President in history. His was also the longest marriage of all Presidents at 77 years. He was the first President to live to see the 40th anniversary of his inauguration.

The oval office was tense on January 19, 1981. Americans were being held captive by the fanatical Iranian clerics who had overthrown the Shah's government. The Americans had been in captivity since November of 1979. Having previously had their hopes dashed numerous times, the President, his staff, and the American public anxiously awaited word from Warren Christopher and the Algerians who were negotiating the release. Success had been achieved. Yet it was bitter sweet for Carter. The release would come at the moment James Earl Carter was handing over the reins of power to the new President, Ronald Reagan. Jimmy Carter was going home to Plains, Georgia.

James Earl "Jimmy" Carter, Jr. was born to Earl and Lillian Carter on October 1, 1924 the eldest of four children in a small town called Plains, Georgia near Americus. Don't be surprised if you haven't heard of this small farming community 158 miles to the south of Atlanta. Plains is the epitome of rural farm-life. Earl Carter was a successful peanut farmer and politician. He had served on the Rural Electrification Board during the Roosevelt years when electricity reached the rural areas of America. He had also served on the local school board, and just a year before his death in 1953, Carter was elected to the Georgia State Legislature.

Miss Lillian Carter

If the future President received his training as a farmer and politician from his father, he gained his humble servant's spirit from his beloved mother Lillian. "Miss Lillian" as many fondly called the matriarch, was delightful, full-spirited and lived long enough to see her son both elected and defeated as President. The former Peace Corp volunteer campaigned vigorously for Jimmy. She lived to be 85 (1983).

As a young man, Jimmy Carter was industrious. He raised peanuts, sold them, and saved the profits until he could buy investments such as rental houses. During his developmental years, Carter was greatly impacted by Julia Coleman, the school superintendent who taught him a love for the arts and for reading. His first major reading assignment was the classic Tolstoy work **War and Peace**. He loved it, and the work became Carter's favorite book beside the Bible. Carter played basketball at Plains High School and was part of the Future Farmers of America.

When time for college arrived, Carter enrolled in Georgia Southwestern and continued his engineering studies at Georgia Tech. He was an excellent student and managed admission to Annapolis where he majored in nuclear fission and both

Julia Coleman

peaceful and destructive usages for the new science. Carter graduated 59th in his class putting him in the top 10%. After his graduation from Annapolis, he continued graduate studies at Union College and served in both the Pacific and Atlantic fleets. Carter came from a long line of military service. His family had been in the new world since the early 1600s and among his ancestors are those who fought in the American Revolutionary War and in the Civil War. Carter went to Annapolis in 1943 and intended to make it his lifelong career. His continual growth in the Navy brought him into the echelons of the frontier technology of nuclear submarines.

As Carter applied for a position in the elite service, the junior officer had to interview with Hyman Rickover, the Captain of the fledgling fleet. In his book **Why Not the Best**, Carter talks about the interview. Rickover asked the young man if he had always done his best. Carter was stunned by the introspection demanded by the question, and he hearkened back to it for his campaign biography published in 1976. Rickover had an immense influence on Carter's life. In the work of nuclear technology there are many dangers. Carter was instrumental in heading the team responding to the meltdown of a reactor at Chalk River in Canada. Carter was well on his way to his ambition of being Chief of Naval Operations, but circumstance precluded that ambition.

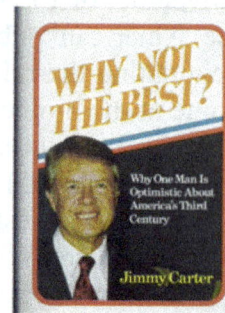

Carter's personal life had also changed during the late forties as he fell in love with and married Eleanor Rosalynn Smith. Her father had died of leukemia when she was barely into her teens, and she had become responsible for helping to raise her siblings. She had known the Carter family as they lived in the same community. But when she saw a picture of Jimmy in his Naval uniform, she fell in love. From this union have come four children: John William "Jack" born in 1947, James Earl "Chip" III born in 1950, Donnell Jeffrey "Jeff" born in 1952 and Amy Lynn born in 1967

The death of Carter's father in 1953 brought an urgent appeal for Jimmy to return to Plains to run the family business. By now Carter was well on his way to building his Naval Career, had a wife and three children, and Rosalynn fiercely objected to him resigning from the Navy to run a peanut farm. But Carter decided to do so. While at first the business was barely making it, so much so that the Carter family moved into public housing to make ends meet, he was intent on making it successful. With a great deal of research, and with Rosalynn working the books to support her husband, soon Jimmy Carter's farm was expanding and doing very well. Even as his father had gained wealth as a farmer, his son found success as well.

Carter in Uniform

Following in his father's footsteps, Carter became very involved in education and the public library system of his community serving on various boards. In 1961, Carter decided to run for the Georgia State Senate. Because of suspected fraud in the election, Carter challenged the results and won! He served two terms in the State Senate where he greatly influenced education laws. Carter was finding that he was part of a new south that was rising from the ashes of segregation. Camelot was in its prime, King was marching with his legions, and the race wars of the south were like a flash fire. But in Jimmy Carter, the Democrats were seeing a rising star of the south, a candidate who championed equal opportunity for all, educational opportunities for the poor, and humanitarianism abroad.

Rosalynn Smith Carter

By 1966, Carter was turning his attention toward Washington, but when the Gubernatorial election in Georgia began to intensify, Carter decided to run for the Democratic nomination. While he came in third in the primary election, he gained enough notice to place him in a good position for the next election. Lester Maddox, a rabid segregationist Democrat, won the election by being chosen by the General Assembly of the state. Carter realized polarizing factions were dividing his home state, and he was determined to bring change to Atlanta. During the next four years, Carter planned strategically and gained momentum. He spoke over 1,000 times throughout the state. He would not be denied. In the election of 1970, Carter ran a vicious primary campaign against former governor Carl Sanders. Some say it smacked of the Dixiecrats message of segregation as he took positions against busing, pro private schools, all positions more akin to the past than to where Carter wanted to lead the state.

Carter won the election even though he refused to be associated with the White supremacy political groups. Even his peanut warehouse was boycotted by these groups. Carter was no segregationist as he was to prove as Governor.

James Earl Carter brought a new idealism to Atlanta. He pressed harder for racial reforms. At the unveiling of a picture of the slain civil rights leader, Martin Luther King, Jr. in the capitol, KKK members protested outside. Carter also pressed for zero based budgeting calling for yearly reviews of every department and program. According to Carter, the mandate helped eliminate 278 of 300 state agencies. With the initial start by the federal government of revenue sharing, Carter was one of a handful of governors to oppose the package of grants from Congress saying "there was no revenue to share."

Maddox

As Carter began to near the end of his term as Governor, having collided with his Lieutenant Governor Maddox on many issues, Carter began to see his image on a national scope. He realized he represented a new south that was rising from a century of rebuilding. Carter began to toy with the idea that he could go further. The aspirant began having conversations with people about what he envisioned for the people of the country. He told of his own poor boy to fame story as the stereotypical American dream. Lawrence Shoup recorded Carter's worth in the mid-seventies as around $5 million. While the Carters had certainly been just farmers, his image of being poor was mildly exaggerated. But the story gained traction.

Governor Carter watched as the nation faltered under the weight and shock of Watergate. In the very year that Richard Nixon resigned, Carter stood before an audience of supporters and with these words announced his candidacy for President. "Hello, I'm Jimmy Carter, and I'm running for President of the United States." Few gave him much of a

Portrait of James Earl Carter as Governor

chance at winning. He would have difficulty gaining the nomination because he was from the south. His campaign biography recaptured a nineteenth century practice that had disappeared from American politics. But many things were happening behind the scenes. As Governor, Carter had been named to Rockefeller's Trilateral Commission, an important think tank. Founded by David Rockefeller, the Trilateral Commission's mission was to bring understanding of cooperation and its benefits between the North America, Europe and Asia. As a candidate, he was receiving support from business and media leaders around the country including CBS, Coca-Cola, and Leonard Woodcock, leader of the UAW. Carter seemed a humble, simple man, and his message resonated with people. He was running as an outsider to help clean up the mess in Washington. He believed the incumbent President, Gerald Ford, was part of the problem. With the faltering economy, inflation, and mistrust in government, Carter believed this strategy would work. In his book, **Why Not the Best**, Carter wrote:

> *The root of the problem is not so much that our people have lost confidence in government, but that government has demonstrated time and again its lack of confidence in the people* (154).

He further stated in his work **A Government as Good as Its People** that *the government can be both competent and compassionate. ... That we could have, and must have, a government as good as its people.* (8)

Carter would have to fend off many prospective candidates for the nomination including California Governor Jerry Brown, Alabama Governor George Wallace (who had come back from a near fatal assassination attempt in 1972), Congressman Mo Udall, Senator Scoop Jackson, Senator Frank Church, Senator Robert Byrd, Ambassador Sargent Shriver, Senator Lloyd Bentsen, and a few lesser known candidates. The field was crowded, but Carter was slowly rising to the top. On the Republican side, Ronald Reagan was challenging for the leadership of the party in what turned out to be a very heated primary season. Most pundits were surprised when Carter won the Iowa caucus and the New Hampshire primary asserting himself as the leading contender for the nomination. And while he was gaining momentum, there were threats to his candidacy.

Billy Carter, Jimmy's younger, beer guzzling brother, was very loud in his support for Jimmy's candidacy, but he wasn't very careful of his language. Meanwhile, Ruth, his evangelist sister drew attention to herself that could be rather unwanted. Miss Lillian was doing what she could for her son, and probably helped him even though she was outspoken. His children and wife were out campaigning hard for his election.

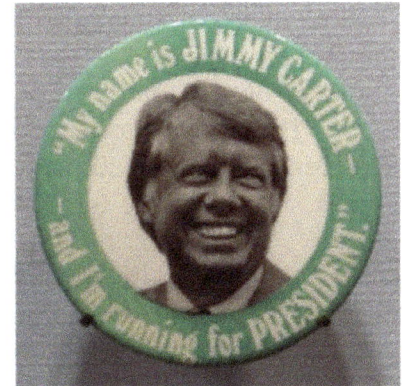

I don't have to be President. There are a lot of things I would not do to be elected. I wouldn't tell a lie. I wouldn't make a misleading statement. I wouldn't betray a trust. I wouldn't avoid a controversial issue. If I do any of those things, don't support me, because I wouldn't deserve to lead this country." (56, **A Government as Good as It's People**)

Summer came, and Carter was nominated. Gerald Ford, the incumbent, received the Republican nomination

11

after a heated battle with Ronald Reagan. The battle lines were clearly drawn. Carter chose Senator Walter Mondale of Minnesota as his running mate. Mondale, cast in the image of Hubert Humphrey, was a known liberal in the party. Ford, who was considered a moderate Republican, chose Senator Bob Dole, a conservative Kansas Republican, to join his ticket having removed from contention Vice President Nelson Rockefeller. It was thought this was an attempt on Ford's part to appease the Reagan conservatives. The truth is that Rockefeller had removed himself from contention.

By Labor Day, Carter had a commanding 30-point lead over President Ford. Ford seemed a very inept campaigner, but not Dole. He became the dominate force in the President's bid to be elected to a full term. Questions continued to rise over the Nixon pardon, his domestic policy and his handling of foreign crises. Carter, however, had his own misstep. The explosive headlines of the Playboy interview hit during the general campaign when Carter admitted that he had lusted after many women in his life. The wheels almost came off the campaign.

Senator Walter Mondale

Ford tried to look Presidential sending out surrogates to campaign while he remained in the White House. (The strategy was dubbed The Rose Garden strategy.) During the debates, Ford seemed inept even getting confused when speaking about foreign policy. When Ford realized it wasn't working, he went out and campaigned vigorously the final two weeks. By November, the polls were unexpectedly close.

When the results were counted, Carter had won 50.1% of the vote (40.8 million votes) to Ford's 48% (39.1 million votes). Carter had carried 23 states plus the District of Columbia although Ford had carried 27 states. In the electoral vote, it was Carter over Ford 297-240. Carter by no means had received a mandate from the people. But Carter had become the first person to unseat an incumbent President since Franklin Roosevelt defeated President Herbert Hoover in 1932. Now the reality set in. Carter had to prepare to govern.

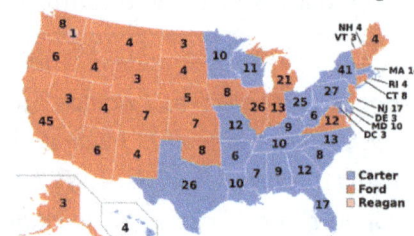

The Carter Presidency was marked by a period of healing from the wounds of Watergate, triumphs in diplomacy, and tremendous failures in domestic policy leading to a time of very high interest rates, inflation, stagnation and unemployment.

President Ford became the first incumbent President defeated since Hoover

> *For myself and for our nation, I want to thank my predecessor for all he has done to heal our land.*
>
> --James Earl Carter, Inaugural Address, Jan 20, 1977

Carter surrounded himself with many colleagues from his Georgia brigade of staffers. He also did well in bringing into the administration many prominent and substantial talents.

Cyrus Vance began the four-year term as Secretary of State, and under his leadership was able to champion diplomacy between Israel and Egypt leading to their peace agreement reached at Camp David. Known as the Camp David Accord, Carter brought Menachem Begin and Anwar Sadat together in secret meetings at the Presidential retreat to talk seriously about peace between the two belligerent countries. When it was announced on September 17, 1978, the international reaction was quick and sharply contrasted the growing divide between the Arab world and the remaining body of nations. Most states applauded the agreement while many Arab nations condemned

Cy Vance

Sadat as a traitor. Carter was praised for his efforts. The Nobel Peace Prize was awarded jointly to Sadat and Begin. But while the agreement was implemented successfully and still holds today, the internal tensions increased in both countries. (Sadat was assassinated in 1981, and Begin would be driven from office in 1983.)

Cy Vance opposed the 1980 rescue mission into Iran and resigned in protest. He was replaced by Senator Edmund Muskie.

Others who served the administration included Michael Blumenthal at Treasury, Harold Brown at Defense, Griffin Bell as Attorney General in the first half of the term followed by Benjamin Civiletti, Joseph Califano at HEW before the beginnings of the Department of Education, and James Schlesinger at the newly formed Department of Energy.

Sadat and Begin after Camp David Accord

The creation of the Departments of Energy and Education were opposed by conservative Republicans who viewed the development as the incursion of big government and an invasion of the rights of states to decide education policy at the local levels. Shirley Hufstedler settled into the new Education cabinet post attempting to strengthen federal regulations and developing monumental education programs with more federal funding but equally more mandates to be implemented by states.

Secretary Hufstedler

Walter Mondale, the new Vice President, served as a close advisor to the President breaking a long string of little used second chairs. Others like under-secretary of state Warren Christopher, who played an important role in negotiations over the Iran hostages, National Security advisor Brzezinski, economic advisor Charles Schultze and others were Washington insiders bringing a sense to many that Carter, while having campaigned for President as an outsider, was now surrounding himself with imminent insiders as well as Georgia staffers from the Governor's office like Jody Powell and Bert Lance. Fellow Georgian and respected Civil Rights leader Andrew Young was appointed the UN Ambassador.

Andrew Young was essential as part of the team that forged Middle East Peace

There were so many issues to be tackled, particularly dealing with the economy, which had faltered horribly under Ford. The country fell into a deep recession. To the country, it appeared that Carter was presiding over a nation going through one crisis after another. The energy crisis that had struck during the Nixon-Ford administration leading to long gas lines, empty pumps and rising fuel costs, diminished little in the early days of Carter's Presidency. This led the President to enact energy policies and move to promote the Department of Energy as a cabinet level position. Carter placed solar panels on the roof of the White House and used the bully pulpit to advise all Americans to turn down their thermostats (as he had in the Executive Mansion). Carter became known for wearing sweaters in the Oval Office.

Carter, who was deeply knowledgeable regarding nuclear energy, had focused the nation on energy issues, but in 1978 he had to deal with nuclear waste and 800 homes that had been built on top of a dump site at Love Canal in New York. Carter convinced Congress to initiate the Superfund for such toxic cleanups.

On the issue of deregulation, the Democratic President appeared to take an unorthodox position favoring the deregulation of many industries which, heretofore, had been under federal guidelines. These industries included the airline industry and the brewing industries. The elimination of airline regulations meant the free market would now determine competition and routes instead of a federal board. It did not diminish safety regulations enforced by the Federal Aviation Administration, but it put the government out of the equation regarding fares and routes.

The deregulation of the brewing industry was the first time since Prohibition that the government did not regulate the sale of hops and other ingredients in the brewing process. If you enjoy the benefits of a growing microbrewery industry in America, you have the Carter Administration to thank for that outcome.

One of the most controversial of Carter's early actions actually happened the day after inauguration day as the President announced the pardon of all Vietnam Era draft dodgers at a VFW convention. Pundits were baffled by his selection of this venue for the announcement. As expected, many staunch war hawks denounced the executive order. But Carter believed if a former President, who had obviously evaded prosecution from high crimes and misconduct in office, could receive the Ford pardon, then those young men who had fled to Canada deserved to return home and allow the nation to heal over the wounds of Vietnam. The nation had transformed to a volunteer military, and Carter was convinced that this action was necessary to continue the healing of festering sores.

Fireside chat from the Library

Carter also believed in communication, although he was rather ineffective as a speaker with a slow, deliberate delivery and heavy Georgia accent. But he hearkened back to the fireside chats of Franklin Roosevelt and believed he could initiate such informal appearing talks in front of the fireplace and be more effective. While his attempt was sincere, it only brought ridicule as an attempt to copy Roosevelt.

In his first year in office, President Carter pursued an issue that split the Republican party between the moderate factions of Gerald Ford and Howard Baker, a leader of Senate Republicans, and the more conservative faction led by former California Governor Ronald Reagan. The government of Panama was asking for full control of the Panama Canal which had been begun by the French in 1904 but finally finished by the United States in 1914. The U.S. had controlled the important waterway since that time. Carter favored handing over the canal to Panamanian control, although the debate was heated in Congress. Conservatives accused Carter, and those who supported the handover, of giving away American territory. (More recently, President Trump has stated his intent on regaining control of the Canal even if it means using the military.)

President Roosevelt had originally made the deal in treaty with Columbia, who actually controlled the land in 1903. The U.S. Senate ratified the treaty, but the Columbian legislature refused to do so. The Hay treaty would grant the United States control and access to the land in perpetuity. When Panama led a separatist revolt against Columbia, Roosevelt sanctioned the usage of American troops to block the Columbian military and quickly recognized the new Panamanian government. They quickly signed the Hay Treaty, and construction commenced the following year. Included in the language was a cycle of re-evaluation of the agreement. When the conversation heated up in Congress, it became evident that Baker would hold a key vote. Even though he was advised

President Carter signing the Panama Canal Treaty

by many not to vote for the agreement, Baker cast the deciding vote in favor of the Panama Canal treaty. His vote was used against him in the Presidential primaries in 1980 by Ronald Reagan. Many insiders believe the Panama vote prevented Howard Baker from winning the Republican nomination in 1980.

Carter achieved a great deal in foreign policy during his four years, but the Iran crisis will forever be the watershed event by which his administration is remembered. It haunted the last year of his Presidency. But other events had not been so dire.

President Nixon successfully opened the world for relations with China bringing the secretive Communist nation into the forefront of countries. His iconic visit to the Great Wall and other images of that historic trip became a great part of Nixon's successful portfolio in foreign policy. Cy Vance, Secretary of State for

Senator Howard Baker

Carter, had for months been in secret negotiations with Chinese officials to normalize relations between the two countries. This hallmark agreement eased tensions between the two powers and helped bring China into a position of stabilizing the region. Despite the loud protests of Ronald Reagan and conservative Republicans, and even a lawsuit by Barry Goldwater, normalization was officially reached on December 14, 1978.

Carter muses in his memoirs about the White House dinner held in China's honor:

> *We had invited both former American Presidents to the formal banquet, and, predictably, the Washington Press was fascinated with the presence of President Nixon in the White House. ... It was obvious from their private comments that for the Chinese he would always be a revered friend... (207-208).*

16

The repercussions of normalization of relations with China meant strained relations with the Soviet Union. Three Mile Island, the nuclear accident, brought greater pressure to reduce nuclear arsenals. Talks had begun on the Strategic Arms Limitation Treaty II soon after the administration took office. Brezhnev, the aging Soviet leader, was in earnest about desiring further reductions. He had previously signed SALT I with President Ford in 1974, but the negotiating was difficult as many snags ensued regarding verification. But by June of 1979, and with the impetus of Three Mile Island fresh in everyone's mind, it was announced that an agreement had been achieved. The treaty was signed on June 18 in Vienna with the two leaders surrounded by a legion of advisors and generals. Carter had stressed in their conversation the importance of reaching an agreement to which the Soviet leader responded *if we do not succeed, God will not forgive us*.

Signing of SALT II Agreement

But the treaty would have difficulty in the American Senate as Republican leader Howard Baker and former Vice-Presidential candidate Bob Dole (both possible candidates for President in 1980), condemned the treaty for lack of verification. The treaty languished in Congress until on December 27, 1979, when a momentous decision by the U.S.S.R. ended consideration of the treaty. The Soviet Union invaded Afghanistan, assassinated their leader, and declared military occupation. The Soviets were roundly condemned for their aggression. SALT II was temporarily withdrawn from consideration. Carter decided that sanctions should be put in place against the Soviet Union.

Russia was deeply in need of American wheat. The President decided to enjoin a grain embargo against the U.S.S.R. Russia was also scheduled to host the 1980 summer Olympics. Amidst a great deal of consternation from critics, Carter announced that U.S. athletes would not be allowed to travel to Moscow. However, the Winter Olympics were being

Miracle on Ice- New York Post, Getty Image

held in Lake Placid, New York. During the games held in February, the United States hockey team shocked the world by beating the Soviet team. Hailed as the *miracle on ice,* the nation embraced these young heroes.

The politics of the Middle East are treacherous at best. Long-term friends can one day be firmly in power and over-night a coup can reduce the nation to chaos. Such was the case of the Shah of Iran. The Shah, and his father before him, had maintained power through ruthlessness. But the world knew of him,

The Shah of Iran

not as a brutal dictator, but as a wealthy, dignified leader of an important Middle Eastern country. When Islamic fanatical clerics toppled his government, the Shah attempted to flee. The militants were led by cleric Ayatollah Khomeini. Eventually the Shah was granted asylum in the United States. Carter seemed to stagger in the weight of these events.

The radicals shouted *death to America*. On November 4, 1979, they stormed the American Embassy and took fifty-two Americans hostage. The nation held its breath. Carter's popularity plummeted. It was, as Carter writes in his diary, apparent that *Khomeini is determined to humiliate America*. When there seems to be any grain of hope for their release, those working with the negotiators for the United States would be replaced. Day after day, the turmoil of Iran was a black cloud over the nation.

Wreckage from Operation Eagle Claw

Between the actions of Russia and those in Iran, the United States was reeling. Carter insisted that draft registration be reinstituted in the US to which Congress quickly acquiesced. In his State of the Union address in January 1980, the President, in a joint session of Congress, articulated the Carter Doctrine which declared that any further encroachment by the Soviet Union into the Persian Gulf region would be considered a threat to our national interest and would be met with military action. A failed rescue mission in April of 1980 supplemented the public perception of incompetence on the part of the President. With an election coming in November, things looked very bleak.

As a repercussion of the Iranian crisis, oil supplies were reduced causing a corresponding increase in inflation. The economic problems worsened to a point unparalleled since the Great Depression. Refugees were pouring in from Cuba and Haiti often causing moments of crisis. Interest rates neared all-time records. Unemployment was creeping higher. By 1980, inflation was at 13.5%. By mid-year, unemployment was at 7.8%. The standard mortgage rate was 13.74% but would go three points higher by the beginning of the Reagan administration.

And in the midst of all of this malaise and crisis of confidence, nature wreaked havoc. On May 19 1980, Mount St. Helens erupted in Washington state. The eruption became the deadliest and costliest in US history. 57 people were killed. Hundreds of homes were destroyed, 40+ bridges were demolished, scores of forests toppled, and miles of highways and railroads suffered destruction. The eruption was so great that it blew off 1300 feet from the summit. The cleanup cost more than 1 billion dollars.

President Carter, despite all the dismal economic news, proposed the first balanced budget since Nixon's second year in office. It was given little chance of passage in Congress due to all the stress on both the economy and the military needs

Mt. Saint Helens

of the time. The budget, some $640 billion, became even larger than was planned.

As the 1980 election drew near, it appeared there would be a bloodbath in the Republican Party as Ronald Reagan, George H. W. Bush, Howard Baker, former Texas Governor John Connally, Illinois Representatives John Anderson and Phil Crane, Connecticut Senator Lowell Weicker, Kansas Senator Bob Dole, and several other candidates fought in bitter primary campaigns for the nomination. Baker was the frontrunner at the outset because of his leadership during the Watergate scandal, but he faltered early and the race narrowed quickly between Reagan and Bush. At the convention, there was talk of Reagan putting Ford on the ticket as his running mate, but in the end, a deal could not be reached, and Reagan selected Bush.

Kennedy DNC 1980 Speech

The Democrats desired to unify behind the incumbent President, but the nation was in such turmoil because of the hostage situation and because of the ineffectiveness of the administration in handling the economy, that Senator Ted Kennedy, the last surviving Kennedy brother, tossed his hat into the fray to try to deny this President the nomination. The primary was contentious and for a time it looked as though Kennedy might be successful. President Carter refused to campaign opting to look Presidential as he continued to work on the release of the hostages. A CBS 60 Minutes interview conducted between Kennedy and Roger Mudd again highlighted past mistakes of Kennedy notably the Chappaquiddick incident in which a young lady was killed. At the convention, Kennedy gave an impassioned speech, but failed to gain the nomination.

In a revolt against the Reagan nomination, populist Representative John Anderson decided to run as a third-party candidate.

President Carter knew he had a tough fight on his hands with the former California Governor. Reagan was popular, conservative, a great contrast with Carter. Reagan campaigned as a fiscal conservative, supporter of a strong military, deeply opposed to communism, and a believer in trickle down economics. He believed the economy was controlled by the wealthy. If you enriched them through tax cuts and breaks, they would bless those below them with an expansion of the economy.

While no flaming liberal, Carter wanted the government to pursue the role of peacemaker and to negotiate reductions in arms. He had championed lowering government spending and waste, but had been hit with bad economic circumstances, much of which was out of his control, like the OPEC actions. Carter decided to campaign in venues generally not used in Presidential politics. Knowing that many college students were fearful that Reagan would promote a return to the draft, Carter made appeals to young people throughout the nation including in Nashville, Tennessee where he appeared on stage with Bill Monroe at the Grand Ole Opry building in front of large group of college students. The author was present for that event on October 9,

1980.

The debates scheduled by the League of Women Voters brought controversy. The League viewed Congressman Anderson as a legitimate candidate and invited him to participate in the debates, one scheduled in September for Baltimore and a second scheduled in Cleveland for October. But President Carter refused to appear in the first debate if Anderson were included. Reagan insisted he would not participate if Anderson were excluded. Reagan and Anderson ended up in a one on one debate without Carter in the Baltimore exchange. Reagan easily handled Anderson who saw his ratings go down after the debate. The second debate was canceled when Carter and Reagan could not come to terms. When Reagan's handlers finally agreed to exclude Anderson, the two met in Cleveland.

Anderson's popular appeal amazed pundits. And in many states, including Tennessee, Massachusetts, North Carolina and Illinois, Reagan, who won all four states, had less than 50% of the votes cast. Anderson had made a huge difference.

When the votes were counted, Reagan had received 50.8% (43.9 million) votes to Carter's 41% (35.4 million). Anderson had received no electoral votes, and had won no states, but he managed to pull 5.7 million votes (6.6%). Most of these were Democratic votes taken away from Carter. Reagan seemed to have benefited most by Anderson's presence. The Reagan revolution not only swept the conservative into the White House, leading to the second defeat of an incumbent President since Hoover, but it swept the Republicans into control of the Senate for the first time since Eisenhower.

On January 20, 1981, as the mantel of power passed from Jimmy Carter to Ronald Reagan, the 444-day hostage ordeal ended as the hostages were handed over and given their freedom. While difficulties with Iran would continue for several decades more, and Reagan would change the political landscape of the world, Jimmy Carter would go back to Plains, Georgia having been rejected by the American people. But he wasn't done with his work.

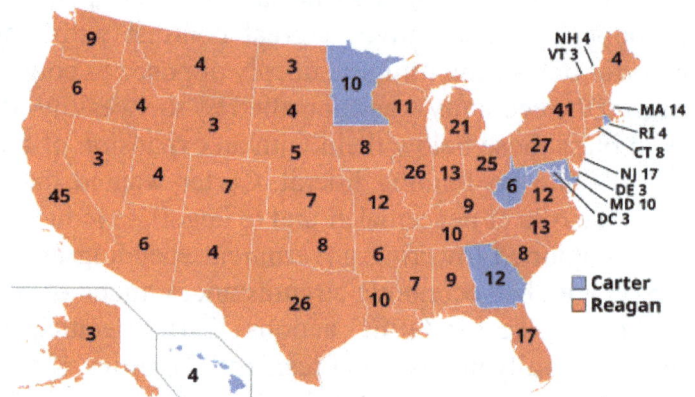

It is generally acknowledged, that Jimmy Carter is the most successful former President in history. His time out of office in "retirement" broke the record set by Herbert Hoover spanning more than two generations. He was the only President to see his 40th year out of office. And he has been exceptionally active having brokered peace agreements, overseen elections in foreign countries, and working through the Carter Center to make a global difference in difficult areas. His writings have been prolific continuing his voice in the social fabric. (See the list of books written at the end of this book.) The Carter Center has actively worked to end disease in many areas of Africa including great success in ending Guinea Worm Disease. The former President continued to press his agenda of human rights even battling his own Baptist denomination over segregated churches. Subsequent Presidents called on him for specific diplomatic missions. Carter was instrumental in the framework of the Geneva Accord to bring peace between Palestinians and Israel. He worked to bring peace and normalization to Haiti, Cuba and Vietnam. His work with Habitat for Humanity has been heavily documented with the former President engaged in building houses.

President Carter became a partner with Nelson Mandela in The Elders, a group of world leaders dedicated to bringing peace to war-torn nations.

Desmond Tutu, Nelson Mandela and Jimmy Carter 2010

At times Carter has criticized the actions of Presidents. He called the Clinton pardon of Marc Rich "disgraceful" and severely criticized President George W Bush's actions in Iraq. During the Obama years he has been very vocal in condemning drone attacks and in continuing to operate the military base at Guantanamo. He played an active role in his Center's activities and trying to make a difference in the world well into his late 90s.

In 2002, Carter became the only former President to receive the Nobel Peace Prize for his activities after leaving office. While three sitting Presidents (Teddy Roosevelt, Woodrow Wilson and Barack Obama) have received the prestigious honor, Carter received his in acknowledgement for a body of work over his life.

Nobel Peace Prize

In the summer of 2015, this author had the privilege of meeting President Carter at a book signing in Nashville, Tennessee. His warm smile still brightens rooms. And while my experience lasted every bit of 15 seconds, I was deeply honored to have been able to see him once again. Just a few days later, on August 12th, President Carter announced that he had been diagnosed with cancer. The former President's treatments were successful. During the course of Covid, President and Mrs. Carter remained primarily in their residence in Plains, Ga, occasionally attending church where he still taught a class until more recent days. One of the final Habitat projects he engaged in was when he was 95 years old.

> **"I have one life and one chance to make it count for something. I'm free to choose that something. That something—the something that I've chosen—is my faith. My faith demands that I do whatever I can, wherever I can, whenever I can, for as long as I can with whatever I have, to try to make a difference."**

Not long after President George H. W. Bush passed away in 2018, President Carter became the oldest living former President. President and Mrs. Carter joined the other former Presidents and President and Mrs. Trump in honoring President Bush at his funeral in the National Cathedral in Washington.

Much of Mrs. Carter's life was spent in an effort to help with mental health awareness. In May of

2023, the Carter Center announced that the former first lady had been diagnosed with dementia. She remained at home, even while her husband was in hospice care. The former President had been in and out of the hospital numerous times and decided earlier in 2023 that he was ready to finish his earthly race. On July 7, 2023, the couple celebrated their 77th wedding anniversary, the longest Presidential marriage in history. On November 19, 2023, Rosalynn Carter passed away. She was honored by the country for her work in mental health and as an esteemed First Lady of Georgia and the nation. She was laid to rest in a place at the residence in the front yard where they had decided to be buried. Their home had already been signed over to the National Park Service to be added to the other historical points in Plains. The Carter Center released the following statement on behalf of President Carter.

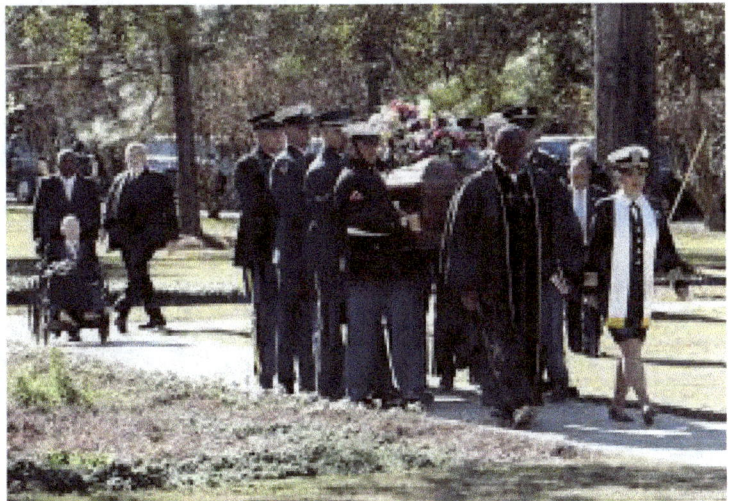

Rosalynn was my equal partner in everything I ever accomplished. She gave me wise guidance and encouragement when I needed it. As long as Rosalynn was in the world, I always knew somebody loved and supported me.

Rosalynn Carter burial in Plains with President Carter following in wheelchair

As the Presidential election of 2024 neared, the President's family released a statement that the former President desired to live long enough to vote for Kamala Harris for President. In October, he did just that. On October 1st, President Carter reached the milestone of his 100th birthday, the only American President to reach the centenarian mark. Only Alf Landon, the 1936 Republican Presidential Candidate, and Jimmy Carter, the 1976 and 1980 Democratic Presidential Candidate have reached the century birthday among Presidential candidates.

On December 29, 2024, President James Earl Carter, Jr. passed into the hands of God. He received tributes from around the globe and was given a full national funeral. All the former Presidents praised this simple man from Plains. President Biden would eulogize him at the National Cathedral. President Carter's coffin would lie in repose at the Carter Center, at the United States Capitol Rotunda before making his journey back to Plains for burial.

Honor guard as President Carter's flag-draped coffin is in the Capitol Rotunda in Washington DC.

President Carter joined 12 other Presidents who have lain in state in the rotunda of the capitol. It is considered an honor bestowed on national leaders allowing the citizens to line up and proceed past the coffin paying their respects. Abraham Lincoln, James Garfield, William McKinley, Warren Harding, William Howard Taft, John F. Kennedy, Herbert Hoover, Dwight Eisenhower, Lyndon Johnson, Ronald Reagan, Gerald Ford, and George H. W. Bush are the other Presidents so honored. Since 1958, the only two Presidents who have not been so honored were Harry Truman and Richard Nixon.

The Carter Center in Atlanta, Georgia

The Carter Center is both the Presidential Library and Museum, and a working organization that works to bring peace to troubled regions of the globe, work with private organizations to bring lifesaving medications to the sick, provide housing, end diseases, and do good. President Carter was very active in the Carter Center up until the last few years of his life. The story is told by his grandson that when the attacks happened in Israel, the former President tried to get up when he heard the reports on television. "What are you doing?" they asked him. "I've got to get to Washington and help them solve this."

A
TOWN MEETING
with
PRESIDENT
JIMMY CARTER

(Doors open at 9:30 a.m. You must be seated by 11 a.m.)

October 9, 1980
Grand Ole Opry House   Admit One
Opryland   № **2263**
Nashville, Tennessee

Paid for and authorized by the Carter/Mondale Re-Election Comm. Inc.

During the 1980 Re-election campaign, I was selected as a college student from David Lipscomb College to attend a Town Hall Meeting at the Grand Ole Opry with President Carter. My ticket. I will never forget being there. There was introductory music by Bill Monroe and his Bluegrass Boys. And then the President was introduced and walked on stage. There was a speech of sorts, but primarily he answered questions.

Replica of Oval Office at Carter Presidential Museum

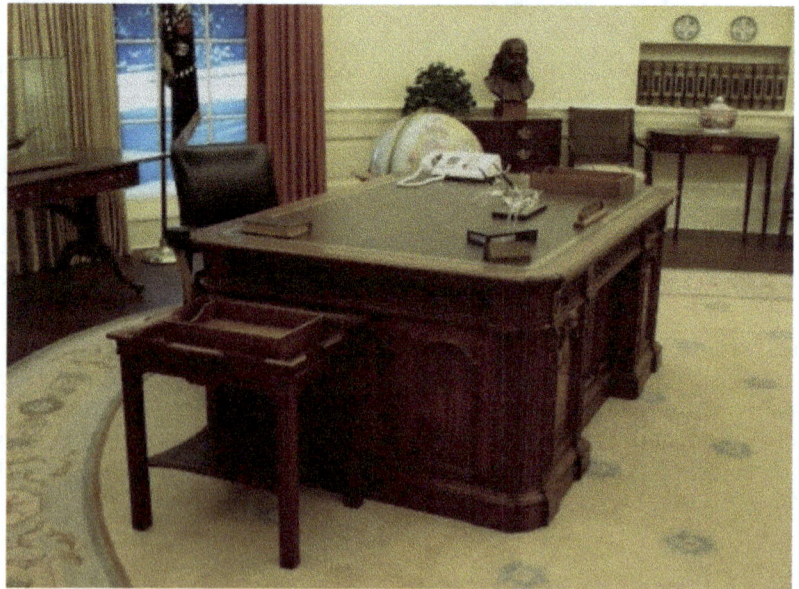

President and Mrs. Carter celebrating their anniversary in 2020. The couple was married for 77 years.

President Carter delivers his inauguration speech, January 20, 1977. Also visible in the picture is Rosalynn Carter, Vice President Walter Mondale, Vice President Hubert Humphrey, Justice Warren Burger, and Vice President Nelson Rockefeller and President Gerald Ford. Amy Carter is beside her mother.

Courtesy Carter Presidential Library, Picture by Words of Wisdom

The incoming and outgoing administration, 1977. President and Mrs. Carter, President and Mrs. Ford, Vice President and Mrs. Rockefeller, Vice President and Mrs. Mondale.

Courtesy Carter Presidential Library, Picture by Words of Wisdom

President Carter dealt with an energy shortage during his Presidency. To help, he lowered the thermostats in the White House to save energy and encouraged others to do the same. To help stay warm, he encouraged wearing sweaters. This is one he wore.
Courtesy Carter Presidential Library. Picture by Words of Wisdom.

An enduring legacy of the Carter Presidency is the need to secure Human Rights for all people throughout the world. This became a part of American foreign policy. It is also a hallmark of the work done by the Carter Center post Presidency. Overseeing elections, brokering peace agreements, and helping societies become healthier and happier was the goal of the 39th President.

Courtesy of the Carter Presidential Library. Picture by Words of Wisdom

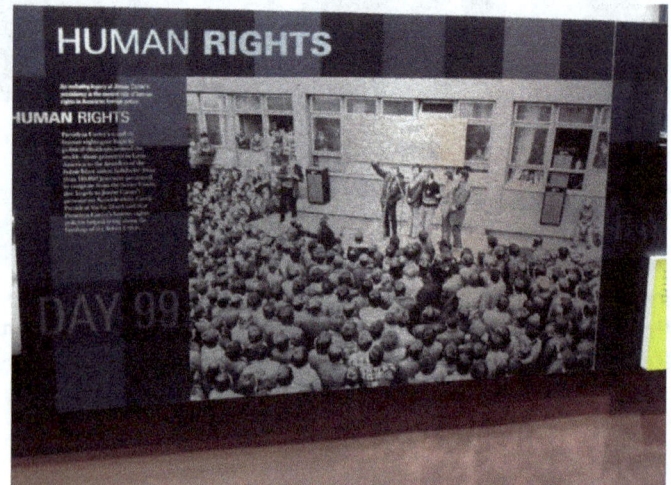

Part of the 32 books written by President Carter in his life. Courtesy Carter Presidential Library, Picture taken by Words of Wisdom

On August 9, 1999, President Bill Clinton award Rosalynn and President Carter the Presidential Medal of Freedom.

Courtesy Carter Presidential Library. Picture taken by Words of Wisdom

In 2007 President Carter received this Grammy Award for Best Spoken Book. *Our Endangered Values: America's Moral Crisis* was the book. It is one of three Grammy Awards received by the former President.

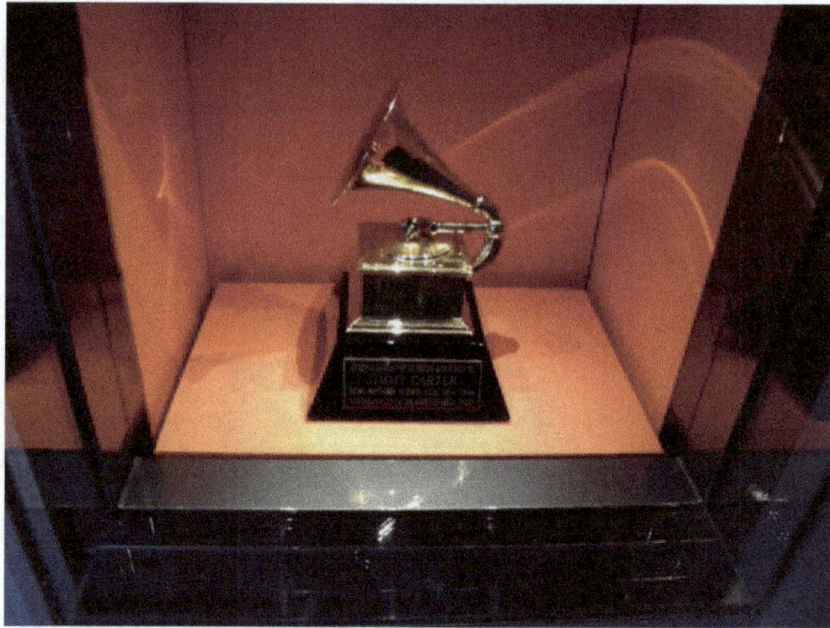

In 2014, I met President Carter at the downtown Nashville Public Library. He was 90 years old, and the smile could still light up a room. He autographed my book. Just a few days after signing the book, President Carter was diagnosed with cancer. He went through treatments and was pronounced cancer free. He would live another 10 years after this event.

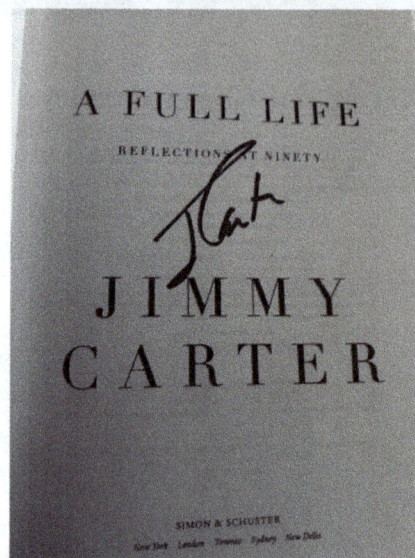

Scenes from the Boyhood Home

The Barn at the Carter Boyhood home was used primarily to house the horses and other animals used for farm work. Jimmy had to work on the farm and would get up early to do the morning chores. The shadow took the picture.

The Dinner bell was not only used to call the folks to eat, but it was also used by the foreman to awaken the sleeping workers

Jimmy Carter Slept Here

Our lives then were centered almost completely around our own family and our own home...

Jimmy Carter, 1975, *Why Not the Best?*

This is the homeplace—"hot in the summer, and cold in the winter"—of a Georgia farmboy who would someday sleep in the White House. Here young Jimmy Carter ran, dodging dogs, chickens, geese, and guinea fowl. The yard was swept white sand, weeded clean to keep snakes and bugs away from the house. Behind you, a woodpile stacked high with hickory, oak, and pine for the fireplaces and kitchen stove took up much of the back yard. A chinaberry tree near the house held a treehouse where Jimmy played.

As you step onto the back porch, listen for the echoes of his father, "Mr. Earl" Carter, hurrying out on some farm business, and his mother, "Miss Lillian," banging the screen door on her way to help someone with her nursing skills. You'd have found the back door unlocked.

Jimmy (far left) and his sisters pose with two friends and Annie Mae Hollis, who often kept the Carter children.

Carter wrote about his life on the farm in his book *Why Not The Best?* This farm was the center of his universe as a child. But he learned life lessons here that blessed him in life and made him the man he became.

33

The boyhood farm is still a working farm, or was while he was living. The Park ranger told me that Mr. Carter had eggs every morning from the chickens on this farm. Upon his passing, the motorcade made a stop at the boyhood home where he spent his early years.

Cash crops at the farm included cotton, corn, watermelons, sugar cane, sweet potatoes, and peanuts.

It was an incredibly tough life involving hundreds of acres of land. This also mean raising food for the family to eat such as in this garden.

Working the farm also required a great deal of equipment. Some of that equipment is still on display. There was plenty of work to be done by hand as well. Unlike a factory job, this one isn't 9-5.

Catch the Mules

Here, at the barn, the day started early.

During the…season all the workers arose each morning at 4:00 a.m.…, wakened by the ringing of a large farm bell. We would go to the barn and catch the mules by lantern light, put the plow stocks, seed, fertilizer, and other supplies on the wagons, and drive out to the field where we would be working that day…and wait for it to be light enough to cultivate…

Jimmy Carter, 1975 *Why Not the Best?*

This 1930s photo of a Georgia barn shows a large bell like the one Jack Clark rang here one hour before daybreak. Although this is not the Carter barn, similar scenes took place here.

Before World War II, mules—not a gasoline-driven tractor—provided the "horsepower" needed to farm in south Georgia.

Jimmy Carter here in 1970. Notice the tractor. During the span of one lifetime, machines had taken the place of mules. The nearby pumphouse and buggy shed also stored tools, harness, and equipment.

In *Why Not the Best?* Carter talks about getting up at 4:00 am with that dinner bell, going to the barn to "catch the mules" and getting everything ready to work the fields as soon as the soon came up and they could see. Here is the President siting on the cast iron caldron with the barn and tractor in the background.

As with any farm, animals are a large part of childhood memories. The Carters would raise many different kinds of animals including goats. There are still goats there on the farm.

Beside the barn where the horses lived is the harness shed. Here they would shoe the horses or mules, fix wagon wheels, and place the harnesses on the horses or mules and mount them to the wagons. The barn loft would also be used for storing hay for the horses. Hay baling was might hard, but necessary work. And there's that big iron caldron. It would be used for many purposes. I suspect it might even have been used making lye soap.

An inside look at the harness barn. Remember that not only was there the work of the farm, but there was the building and maintaining of all the out buildings like this shed. This buggy and wagon were not made for comfort but for the ability to get from one place to the other. Notice the wheels are wooden.

This seems really foreign to many people today. But keep in mind that President Carter was born in 1924. Wagons and buggies would have definitely been used out in the country on the farm particularly, and even by families in traveling to town or church.

This is one of the most interesting things about the farm. James Earl, Sr. had learned about using wind energy to pump water out of the ground. Wells, generally, had hand pumps. But this one operated via a wind mill system. And, at some point, he had the water pumped into the house. This wind powered well was still operational when the author visited the house and was still pumping water. As the information board says, he erected this in 1935.

This is the restored home of Jack Clark. The move has been moved back from the road a bit. Jack was the farm overseer. He had charge of overseeing that all the work was done and keeping tabs on all the comings and goings on the farm. You'll notice the large metal cooking vat turned upside down under the tree.

The milking barn. On a farm such as this, having cows for milk and beef cows was important to sustain the family and also to have product with which to barter. The cream would also be important. And churning butter and making cheese would also be very useful.

Out in the country, hunting, fishing and tennis were the big outdoor activities. The Carters actually had a clay court on which to play. President Carter loved Tennis. While in the White House, President Carter would work up a game of tennis as often as possible. Below he is playing with Hamilton Jordan his Chief of Staff.

Carter was an avid sports enthusiast, but his favorite sport to play was tennis. He was also an avid runner, liked baseball, and Jimmy and Rosalynn even got caught on the Kiss Cam at an Atlanta Braves game.

Courtesy AP/David Goldman

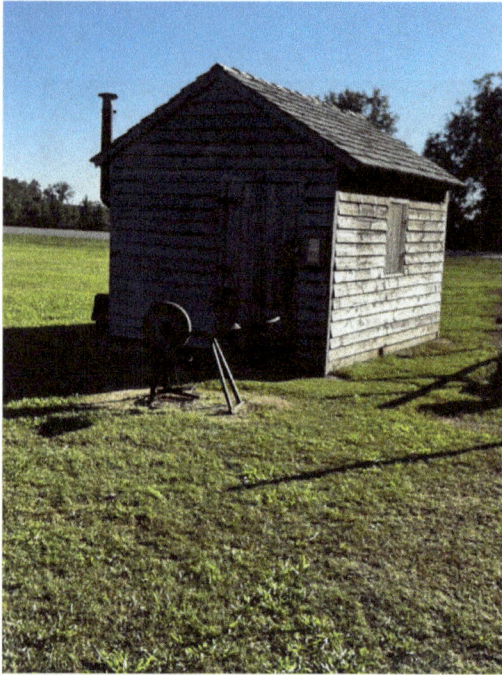

I'm assuming this might well be the smoke house. Out in the country, many farmers smoked their own meats for preservation and then would wrap them and hang them on hooks in little buildings like this.

Sheds would have been common on farms. It was generally a place for placing tools like hammers, pliers, post hole differs, shovels, rakes, all the things one would need to do farm and yard work.

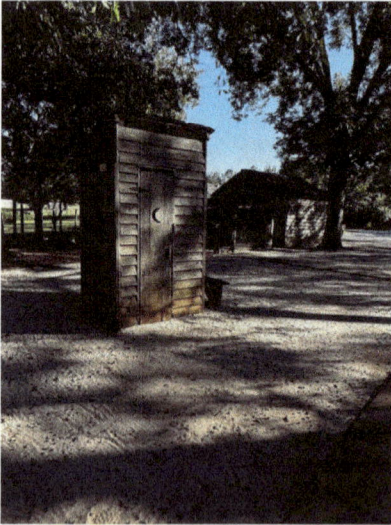

The outhouse was an important part of country living. One would dig a large pit and set this house with its stool on top of the whole. There would be a bit of light that would come in at the top and the moon through the door was so you could tell if there was anyone in there in case they forgot to lock the door. One had to be careful of snakes and wasps as they seemed to like these places. You'll notice the white sand yard. I'm told by the park folks that the white sand was preferred because it allowed easier sighting of snakes. They would rake the sand and sweep it. Back behind this, I believe is the chick house. And yes, there were chickens in there. Both were just a short walk out the back door.

Some might wonder if they went out there to the outhouse at night. The answer is no. They would generally have porcelain "slop" jars in the house they would use at night. These had to be emptied and cleaned in the mornings. Aren't you thankful for your indoor plumbing?

President Carter's Boyhood Home

Earl Carter bought this home in 1928 when Jimmy was just 4 years old. He lived here until he left for College. The House had been built in 1922.

There is still sugar cane on this farm. The NPS has attempted to give the visitor an idea of just what it was like to live on this farm as possible.

A visitor to the boyhood home will be able to walk the very grounds that Jimmy Carter walked, tour the house where he lived from the time he was 4 years old until he went off to College, see the animals who live here, see the crops still being grown, and in general hear stories about the farming life of a rural Georgia family. For more information, be sure to visit the website for the National Park Service. They operate the site and do an amazing job.

Scenes from Plains

Plains is mighty proud of their home town hero. A city located in Sumter County, Georgia about 120 miles south of Atlanta. The population of Plains, as of 2020 was 573. The City was incorporated in 1896. On the main roadway, next to the railroad tracks in what is downtown Plains, there is this monument in honor of their favorite son, Jimmy Carter.

The Old Plains High School where Carter graduated in 1941 is now the Visitor Center for the Jimmy Carter sites. It houses a museum and information about the 39th President.

The typical classroom of the south during the depression years of the 1930s. The desks were always wooden. The tops would sometimes rise in order to store your books and work inside. Teachers used chalkboards in those days. The teacher's desk was almost always front and center in the classroom. There were always American flags present. And often there would be a picture of the current President in the room. In this one replica classroom we see a portrait of George Washington.

Jimmy Carter graduated from High School in Plains in the Class of 1941. Can you tell which one of these students is the future President?

The Plains High School class of 1941. Can you spot Jimmy Carter?

This office was shared by the Principle of the school as well as the superintendent Julia Coleman. Carter would write later that Miss Coleman had a great impact on his life.

INSIDE THE PRINCIPAL'S OFFICE

You have entered where no student wants to be sent: the principal's office.

From this room, Plains High School Superintendent Julia Coleman and Principal Y. T. Sheffield led one of Georgia's best schools in the early 1900s. Students like young Jimmy Carter and Rosalynn Smith called them "Miss Julia" and "Mr. Sheffield." The teaching duo shared this office for over 30 years.

Can you picture them sitting here, perhaps debating student discipline or grading term papers?

After Miss Julia retired in 1938, Mr. Sheffield served as school superintendent until 1945.

Plains to Celebrate 'Julia Coleman Day'

Miss Julia served as a PHS teacher and superintendent. In 1956, the town honored their beloved educator with her very own holiday.

Us older folks know this as a manual typewriter. Many of us perhaps learned to type on one of these. It worked by striking a letter on the keyboard and it would raise a metal piece from the center striking the ribbon and imprinting the raised letter onto the page. If you made a mistake, you had liquid white out. You used carbon paper to make duplicates. This model is on a small desk in the Principle's office.

These store fronts constitute the bulk of downtown Plains. And they let you know it is the home of President Carter. It includes a store once run by family members, and other places to shop. And the one thing they all have in common...they all know the Carters.

Plains Baptist Church was a central part of his life growing up and as an adult. He would leave there over segregation and join the Maranatha Baptist Church.

The Train Depot was used as headquarters for his state Senate, Gubernatorial and Presidential campaigns.

As the author walked through the area, I couldn't help but think how much of what is now Plains is connected to the preservation of the Carter legacy. They are proud to be the hometown of an American President. But one gets the feeling that there is more to it than that. They really love the former President. And there is one simple reason...he was one of them. No show. No flash. He'd wear jeans and hammer together a house with the best of them. President Carter loved writing and woodworking. And he loved going the short distance into downtown to be among his people. Outside of his military career and serving as Governor and President, Jimmy Carter never lived anywhere else. When he was defeated in 1980 by Ronald Reagan, there was never a question as to where he would go. Plains. That's home. He bought his home in Plains in 1961. He never owned another.

Brother Billy Carter's Gas Station was located in the heart of Plains. A block from the High School. Across the street from the train depot. Right next to the police department. And just across the tracks from downtown.

From the Museum

These tools were used by the Carters in their work with Habitat for Humanity. The former President helped to build houses for needy families for much of his adult life. It was one of his fondest charities. And it was President Carter who brought this remarkable work to the forefront in American life. Today, Habitat boasts a lot of volunteers. Generally, Habitat for Humanity operates in some 70 countries. Over the period from 1976, the organization has helped more than 62 million people.

This beautiful quilt is referred to as the Habitat for Humanity Quilt. It was presented to President Carter for his 75th birthday.

Replica of the Resolute Desk and the Seal of the President rug

Grave of first brother Billy Carter

Graves of parents Earl and Lillian Carter and brother Billy.
These are located at the Lebanon Cemetery just out from Plains

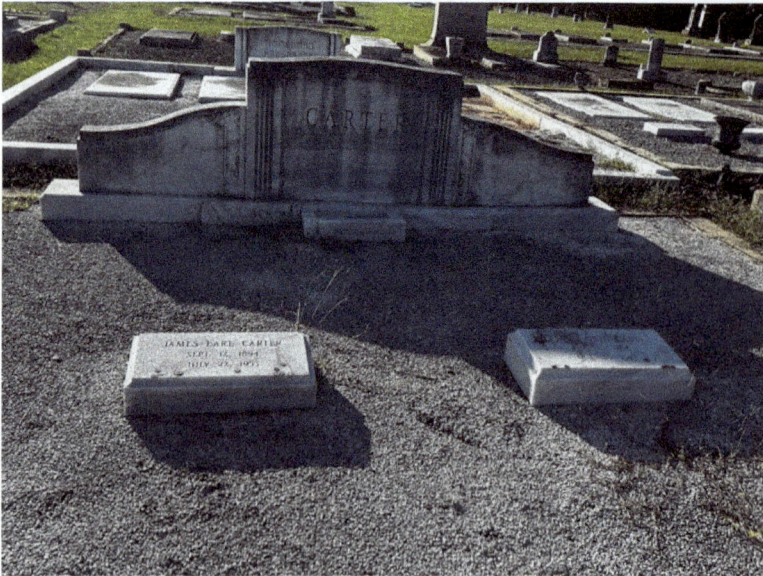

President and Mrs. Carter stunned everyone by getting out of the car and walking down Pennsylvania Ave. during the inaugural parade. Courtesy The Carter Center

President Carter in the Oval Office with Vice President Mondale, Hamilton Jordan and other advisors as he works on negotiations for the hostages being held in Iran.

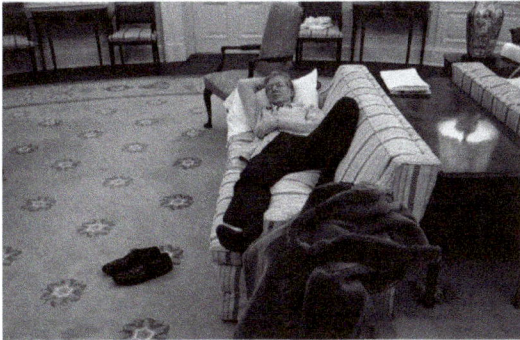

President Carter would often sleep in the Oval Office during the hostage Crisis. He worked some long hours trying to free those Americans being held by the Iranians.

The Carter House in Plains Georgia--The Only House the Carters Ever Owned

JAMES EARL CARTER, JR.
OCT. 1, 1924 — DEC. 29, 2024

GEORGIA STATE SENATOR
GOVERNOR OF GEORGIA
PRESIDENT OF THE UNITED STATES
CO—FOUNDER OF THE CARTER CENTER

Inaugural Address of Jimmy Carter

THURSDAY, JANUARY 20, 1977

For myself and for our Nation, I want to thank my predecessor for all he has done to heal our land.

In this outward and physical ceremony, we attest once again to the inner and spiritual strength of our Nation. As my high school teacher, Miss Julia Coleman, used to say: "We must adjust to changing times and still hold to unchanging principles."

Here before me is the Bible used in the inauguration of our first President, in 1789, and I have just taken the oath of office on the Bible my mother gave me a few years ago, opened to a timeless admonition from the ancient prophet Micah:

"He hath showed thee, O man, what is good; and what doth the Lord require of thee, but to do justly, and to love mercy, and to walk humbly with thy God." (Micah 6: 8)

This inauguration ceremony marks a new beginning, a new dedication within our Government, and a new spirit among us all. A President may sense and proclaim that new spirit, but only a people can provide it.

Two centuries ago our Nation's birth was a milestone in the long quest for freedom, but the bold and brilliant dream which excited the founders of this Nation still awaits its consummation. I have no new dream to set forth today, but rather urge a fresh faith in the old dream.

Ours was the first society openly to define itself in terms of both spirituality and of human liberty. It is that unique self- definition which has given us an exceptional appeal, but it also imposes on us a special obligation, to take on those moral duties which, when assumed, seem invariably to be in our own best interests.

You have given me a great responsibility--to stay close to you, to be worthy of you, and to exemplify what you are. Let us create together a new national spirit of unity and trust. Your strength can compensate for my weakness, and your wisdom can help to minimize my mistakes.

Let us learn together and laugh together and work together and pray together, confident that in the end we will triumph together in the right.

The American dream endures. We must once again have full faith in our country--and in one another. I believe America can be better. We can be even stronger than before.

Let our recent mistakes bring a resurgent commitment to the basic principles of our Nation, for we know that if we despise our own government we have no future. We recall in special times when we have stood briefly, but magnificently, united. In those times no prize was beyond our grasp.

But we cannot dwell upon remembered glory. We cannot afford to drift. We reject the prospect of failure or mediocrity or an inferior quality of life for any person. Our Government must at the same time be both competent and compassionate.

We have already found a high degree of personal liberty, and we are now struggling to enhance equality of opportunity. Our commitment to human rights must be absolute, our laws fair, our natural beauty preserved; the powerful must not persecute the weak, and human dignity must be enhanced.

We have learned that "more" is not necessarily "better," that even our great Nation has its recognized limits, and that we can neither answer all questions nor solve all problems. We cannot afford to do everything, nor can we afford to lack boldness as we meet the future. So, together, in a spirit of individual sacrifice for the common good, we must simply do our best.

Our Nation can be strong abroad only if it is strong at home. And we know that the best way to enhance freedom in other lands is to demonstrate here that our democratic system is worthy of emulation.

To be true to ourselves, we must be true to others. We will not behave in foreign places so as to violate our rules and standards here at home, for we know that the trust which our Nation earns is essential to our strength.

The world itself is now dominated by a new spirit. Peoples more numerous and more politically aware are craving and now demanding their place in the sun--not just for the benefit of their own physical condition, but for basic human rights.

The passion for freedom is on the rise. Tapping this new spirit, there can be no nobler nor more ambitious task for America to undertake on this day of a new beginning than to help shape a just and peaceful world that is truly humane.

We are a strong nation, and we will maintain strength so sufficient that it need not be proven in combat--a quiet strength based not merely on the size of an arsenal, but on the nobility of ideas.

We will be ever vigilant and never vulnerable, and we will fight our wars against poverty, ignorance, and injustice--for those are the enemies against which our forces can be honorably marshaled.

We are a purely idealistic Nation, but let no one confuse our idealism with weakness.

Because we are free we can never be indifferent to the fate of freedom elsewhere. Our moral sense dictates a clear-cut preference for these societies which share with us an abiding respect for individual human rights. We do not seek to intimidate, but it is clear that a world which others can dominate with impunity would be inhospitable to decency and a threat to the well-being of all people.

The world is still engaged in a massive armaments race designed to ensure continuing equivalent strength among potential adversaries. We pledge perseverance and wisdom in our efforts to limit the world's armaments to those necessary for each nation's own domestic safety. And we will move this year a step toward ultimate goal--the elimination of all nuclear weapons from this Earth. We urge all other people to join us, for success can mean life instead of death.

Within us, the people of the United States, there is evident a serious and purposeful rekindling of confidence. And I join in the hope that when my time as your President has ended, people might say this about our Nation:

- that we had remembered the words of Micah and renewed our search for humility, mercy, and justice;

- that we had torn down the barriers that separated those of different race and region and religion, and where there had been mistrust, built unity, with a respect for diversity;

- that we had found productive work for those able to perform it;

- that we had strengthened the American family, which is the basis of our society;

- that we had ensured respect for the law, and equal treatment under the law, for the weak and the powerful, for the rich and the poor;

- and that we had enabled our people to be proud of their own Government once again.

I would hope that the nations of the world might say that we had built a lasting peace, built not on weapons of war but on international policies which reflect our own most precious values.

These are not just my goals, and they will not be my accomplishments, but the affirmation of our Nation's continuing moral strength and our belief in an undiminished, ever-expanding American dream.

The Storming of the American Embassy that began the hostage crisis in Tehran, Iran.

Late yesterday, I cancelled a carefully planned operation which was underway in Iran to position our rescue team for later withdrawal of American hostages, who have been held captive there since November 4. Equipment failure in the rescue helicopters made it necessary to end the mission.

As our team was withdrawing, after my order to do so, two of our American aircraft collided on the ground following a refueling operation in a remote desert location in Iran. Other information about this rescue mission will be made available to the American people when it is appropriate to do so.

There was no fighting; there was no combat. But to my deep regret, eight of the crewmen of the two aircraft which collided were killed, and several other Americans were hurt in the accident. Our people were immediately airlifted from Iran. Those who were injured have gotten medical treatment, and all of them are expected to recover.

No knowledge of this operation by any Iranian officials or authorities was evident to us until several hours after all Americans were withdrawn from Iran.

Our rescue team knew and I knew that the operation was certain to be difficult and it was certain to be dangerous. We were all convinced that if and when the rescue operation had been commenced that it had an excellent chance of success. They were all volunteers; they were all highly trained. I met with their leaders before they went on this operation. They knew then what hopes of mine and of all Americans they carried with them.

To the families of those who died and who were wounded, I want to express the admiration I feel for the courage of their loved ones and the sorrow that I feel personally for their sacrifice.

The mission on which they were embarked was a humanitarian mission. It was not directed against Iran; it was not directed against the people of Iran. It was not undertaken with any feeling of hostility toward Iran or its people. It has caused no Iranian casualties.

Planning for this rescue effort began shortly after our Embassy was seized, but for a number of reasons, I waited until now to put those rescue plans into effect. To be feasible, this complex operation had to be the product of intensive planning and intensive training and repeated rehearsal. However, a resolution of this crisis through negotiations and with voluntary action on the part of the Iranian officials was obviously then, has been, and will be preferable.

This rescue attempt had to await my judgment that the Iranian authorities could not or would not resolve this crisis on their own initiative. With the steady unraveling of authority in Iran and the mounting dangers that were posed to the safety of the hostages themselves and the growing realization that their early release was highly unlikely, I made a decision to commence the rescue operations plans.

This attempt became a necessity and a duty. The readiness of our team to undertake the rescue made it completely practicable. Accordingly, I made the decision to set our long-developed plans into operation. I ordered this rescue mission prepared in order to safeguard American lives, to protect America's national interests, and to reduce the tensions in the world that have been caused among many nations as this crisis has continued.

It was my decision to attempt the rescue operation. It was my decision to cancel it when problems developed in the placement of our rescue team for a future rescue operation. The responsibility is fully my own.

In the aftermath of the attempt, we continue to hold the Government of Iran responsible for the safety and for the early release of the American hostages, who have been held so long. The United States remains determined to bring about their safe release at the earliest date possible.

As President, I know that our entire Nation feels the deep gratitude I feel for the brave men who were prepared to rescue their fellow Americans from captivity. And as President, I also know that the Nation shares not only my disappointment that the rescue effort could not be mounted, because of mechanical difficulties, but also my determination to persevere and to bring all of our hostages home to freedom.

We have been disappointed before. We will not give up in our efforts. Throughout this extraordinarily difficult period, we have pursued and will continue to pursue every possible avenue to secure the release of the hostages. In these efforts, the support of the American people and of our friends throughout the world has been a most crucial element. That support of other nations is even more important now.

We will seek to continue, along with other nations and with the officials of Iran, a prompt resolution of the crisis without any loss of life and through peaceful and diplomatic means.

Thank you very much.

List of Cabinet Members who served in the Carter White House

Secretary of State-	Cyrus Vance
	Edmund Muskie
Secretary of Treasury-	W. Michael Blumenthal
	G. William Miller
Secretary of Defense-	Harold Brown
Attorney General-	Griffin Bell
	Benjamin Civiletti
Secretary of the Interior-	Cecil Andrus
Secretary of Agriculture-	Robert Bergland
Secretary of Commerce-	Juanita Kreps
Secretary of Labor-	Ray Marshall
Secretary of Health, Education, and Welfare-	Joseph Califano, Jr.
	Patricia Harris
Secretary of Health and Human Services-	Patricia Harris
Secretary of Housing and Urban Development-	Patricia Harris
	Maurice "Moon" Landrieu
Secretary of Transportation-	Brock Adams
	Neil Goldschmidt
Secretary of Energy-	James R. Schlesinger
	Charles Duncan, Jr.
Secretary of Education-	Shirley Hufstedler
Director of Office of Management and Budget-	Bert Lance
	James T. McIntyre
United States Trade Representative-	Robert Strauss
	Rubin Askew
Ambassador to the United Nations-	Andrew Young
	Donald McHenry
National Security Advisor-	Zbigniew Brzezinski
Chair of the Council of Economic Advisors-	Charles Schultze

List of the Books Written by President Jimmy Carter during his life

Palestine: Peace Not Apartheid
An Hour Before Daylight: Memories of a Rural Boyhood
A Full Life: Reflections at Ninety
Our Endangered Values: America's Moral Crisis
Faith: A Journey for All
The Virtues of Aging
A Call to Action: Women, Religion, Violence, and Power
The Hornet's Nest: A Novel of the Revolutionary War
White House Diary
Keeping Faith: Memories of a President
Living Faith
Always a Reckoning and Other Poems
Christmas in Plains
The Little Baby Snoogle-Fleejer
Everything to Gain: Making the Most of the Rest of Your Life
Sources of Strength: Meditations on Scripture for a Living Faith
100 Years of Fishing: The Ultimate Tribute to Our Fishing Tradition (Contributor)
The Blood of Abraham: Insights into the Middle East
We Can Have Peace in the Holy Land: A Plan That Will Work
Through the Year with the President: 366 Daily Meditations from the 39th President
A Remarkable Mother
Beyond the White House: Waging Peace, Fighting Disease, Building Hope
Why Not the Best? The First Fifty Years
Turning Point: A Candidate, a State, and a Nation Come of Age
Sharing Good Times
An Outdoor Journal: Adventures and Reflections
Talking Peace: A Vision for the Next Generation
The Art of the Fishing Fly (wrote Introduction)
The Making of the National Parks: An American Idea (Wrote Foreword)
A Government as Good as It's People
The Paintings of Jimmy Carter
The Personal Beliefs of Jimmy Carter: Winner of the 2002 Nobel Peace Prize
The Nobel Peace Prize Lecture
NIV Lessons from Life Bible: Personal Reflections with Jimmy Carter
Negotiation: The Alternative to Hostility

References for Jimmy Carter

Abernathy, M. Glenn, Dilys M. Hill, & Phil Williams, eds. (1984). **The Carter Years: The President and Policy Making**. New York: St. Martin's Press

Anderson, Patrick. (1994) **Electing Jimmy Carter: The Campaign of 1976**. Baton Rouge, LA: Louisiana State University Press.

Bird, Kai. (2021). **The Outlier: The Unfinished Presidency of Jimmy Carter.** New York: Crown.

Bourne, Peter G. (1997). **Jimmy Carter: A Comprehensive Biography from Plains to Postpresidency.** New York: Scribner.

Carter, Jeff (2017). **Ancestors of Jimmy and Rosalynn Carter.** Jefferson, NC: McFarland & Company.

Carter, Jimmy. (1975). **Why Not the Best?** Nashville, TN: Broadman Press.

Carter, Jimmy. (1977). **A Government as Good as its People.** New York: Simon and Schuster.

Carter, Jimmy. (1982). **Keeping Faith**. Toronto, Canada: Bantam Books.

Carter, Jimmy. (2001). **An Hour Before Daylight: Memories of a Rural Boyhood.** New York: Simon & Schuster.

Carter, Jimmy. (2003). **The Hornet's Nest: A Novel of the Revolutionary War.** New York: Simon & Schuster.

Carter, Jimmy. (2004). **Sharing Good Times**. New York: Simon & Schuster.

Carter, Jimmy. (2007). **Beyond the White House: Waging Peace, Fighting Disease, Building Hope.** New York: Simon & Schuster.

Carter, Jimmy. (2010). **White House Diary.** New York: Farrar, Straus, and Giroux.

Carter, Jimmy. (2015). **A Full Life: Reflections at Ninety.** New York: Simon & Schuster.

Carter, Rosalynn. (1984). **First Lady from Plains.** New York: Fawcett.

Eizenstat, Stuart E. (2018). **President Carter: The White House Years.** New York: Thomas Dunne Books.

Knight, Russell (2024). **The Untold Story of President Jimmy Carter: The Humble Humanitarian Who Changed the World.** Knight.

Life (2025). **Jimmy Carter: A Noble Life 1924-2024.** New York: Life.

Miller, William Lee. (1978). **Yankee from Georgia: The Emergence of Jimmy Carter**. New York: Times Books.

Shoup, Lawrence H. (1980). **The Carter Presidency and Beyond: Power Politics in the 1980s.** Palo Alto, CA: Ramparts Press.

Zelizer, Julian E. **Jimmy Carter**. (American Presidents) (2010). New York: Henry Holt.

Photographic Credits

Sadat and Begin Camp David Accords, Library of Congress, Public Domain

Secretary Shirley Hufstedler, Library of Congress, Public Domain

Ambassador Andrew Young, Courtesy Andrew Young Center, Public Domain

President Carter's Fireside Chat, Courtesy National Archives, White House Photograph, Public Domain

Signing of the Panama Canal Treaty, National Archives, White House Photograph, Public Domain

Senator Howard Baker, 1979, by Bernard Gotfryd, Library of Congress, Public Domain

Signing of SALT II Agreement by Bill Fitzpatrick, Public Domain

Shah of Iran, Ghazarians, Public Domain

Miracle on Ice Hockey Match United States vs Russia, New York Post, Getty Image

Wreckage from Operation Eagle Claw, 1980, US Military, Public Domain

Mount St. Helens, United States Geological Survey, Public Domain

Ted Kennedy 1980 DNC Convention Speech, retrieved from tedkennedy.org

President Jimmy Carter and Bill Monroe at the Grand Ole Opry House, October 1980, Storytellers Facebook Post

President Carter Debates Ronald Reagan, 28 October 1980, Courtesy Jimmy Carter Library, Public Domain

Electoral Map 1980 Presidential Election, Wikipedia, SteveSims

The Elders, Tutu, Carter, Mandela, 2010, retrieved from theelders.org.

Rosalynn and Jimmy Carter Building Habitat for Humanity House, Habitat for Humanity Facebook Page, November 2023 Post

Nobel Peace Prize, courtesy Carter Presidential Museum, 2013 ©Words of Wisdom

President Carter Receives the Nobel Peace Prize, 2002, Courtesy The Carter Center

President and Rosalynn Carter, unknown photography, Courtesy The Carter Center

Burial Service for Rosalynn Carter with President Carter in wheelchair, Courtesy The Carter Center

President Carter Lies in State at the Capitol Rotunda, January 7, 2025, Aaron Troutman, US Army, Public Domain

Carter Presidential Center, 2013 ©Words of Wisdom

Ticket to Campaign Event 1980 ©Words of Wisdom

Replica of Oval Office, courtesy Carter Presidential Museum, 2013 ©Words of Wisdom

President and Mrs. Carter anniversary, courtesy The Carter Center. 2020.

President Carter Delivers Inaugural Address, January 20, 1977, Courtesy Carter Presidential Library, ©2014 Words of Wisdom

The Incoming and Outgoing Administration, January 20, 1977, Courtesy Carter Presidential Library, ©2014 Words of Wisdom

Sweater Worn by President Carter, Courtesy Carter Presidential Library, ©2014 Words of Wisdom

Human Rights, Courtesy Carter Presidential Library, ©2014 Words of Wisdom

Books Written, Courtesy Carter Presidential Library, ©2014 Words of Wisdom

Presidential Medals of Freedom, Courtesy Carter Presidential Library, ©2014 Words of Wisdom

Grammy Award, Courtesy Carter Presidential Library, ©2014 Words of Wisdom

Presidential Autograph, ©2014 Words of Wisdom

Scenes from Carter Boyhood

Barn, ©2024 Words of Wisdom

Dinner Bell ©2024 Words of Wisdom

Jimmy Carter Slept Here ©2024 Words of Wisdom

Cash Crops ©2024 Words of Wisdom

Farm Tools ©2024 Words of Wisdom

Catch the Mules ©2024 Words of Wisdom

Goat on Farm ©2024 Words of Wisdom

Harness Shed ©2024 Words of Wisdom

Wagons in Harness Shed ©2024 Words of Wisdom

Wind Powered Well, ©2024 Words of Wisdom

Jack Clark House, ©2024 Words of Wisdom
Milking Barn, ©2024 Words of Wisdom
Tennis Court, ©2024 Words of Wisdom
President Carter and Hamilton Jordan Playing Tennis, Courtesy of the Carter Presidential Library, Public Domain
Carters at a Braves Game, AP/David Goldman
Smoke House, ©2024 Words of Wisdom
Shed on Farm, ©2024 Words of Wisdom
Outhouse, ©2024 Words of Wisdom
President Carter's Boyhood Home, ©2024 Words of Wisdom
Sugar Cane at the Farm, ©2024 Words of Wisdom
Downtown Plains Monument to Carter, ©2024 Words of Wisdom
Old Plains High School-Visitor Center, ©2024 Words of Wisdom
Typical Classroom- ©2024 Words of Wisdom
Class of 1941, Courtesy Plains Visitor Center Museum, ©2024 Words of Wisdom
Principle's Office, ©2024 Words of Wisdom
Manual Typewriter, ©2024 Words of Wisdom
Carter Banner Downtown Plains and Storefronts, ©2024 Words of Wisdom
Plains Baptist Church, ©2024 Words of Wisdom
Train Depot Campaign Headquarters, ©2024 Words of Wisdom
Billy Carter Service Station, ©2024 Words of Wisdom
Habitat Tools Used by the Carters, ©2024 Words of Wisdom
Quilt made by Habitat for Humanity for President Carter's 75th Birthday, ©2024 Words of Wisdom
Replica of Resolute Desk and Presidential Seal Rug, ©2024 Words of Wisdom
Grave of Billy Carter, Lebanon Cemetery, ©2024 Words of Wisdom
Graves of Earl and Lillian Carter, Lebanon Cemetery, ©2024 Words of Wisdom
President and Mrs. Carter Walking during Inaugural Parade, Courtesy The Carter Center, Facebook Page
Meeting with Advisors During Iran Hostage Crisis, Courtesy The Carter Center
Sleeping on Couch in Oval Office During Iran Crisis, Courtesy The Carter Center
Home of President and Mrs. Carter in Plains, Georgia, Library of Congress, Public Domain
Gravesite of President Carter, National Park Service, Laura Kuyat, Public Domain
Storming the Embassy in Tehran, Iran, 4 November 1979, unknown author, Public Domain

Websites for Jimmy Carter
http://www.whitehouse.gov/about/presidents/jimmycarter White House Website on Jimmy Carter
http://www.cartercenter.org/index.html The Carter Center website
http://www.jimmycarterlibrary.gov/ Jimmy Carter Presidential Library and Museum
http://www.pbs.org/wgbh/americanexperience/films/carter/ PBS website
http://millercenter.org/president/carter Miller Center site for Jimmy Carter
http://www.biography.com/people/jimmy-carter-9240013 Biography site on Carter
http://www.nps.gov/jica/index.htm Plains National Park Historic Site
http://www.rollingstone.com/politics/news/the-riddle-of-jimmy-carter-20110201 Interesting Rolling Stone article on Carter
http://theelders.org/jimmy-carter The Elders website
http://www.habitat.org/how/carter.aspx The Carters work with Habitat for Humanity
http://www.history.com/topics/us-presidents/jimmy-carter History channel website

Acknowledgements

President Jimmy Carter was an incredible individual. Thousands of persons have journeyed to Plains, Georgia to attend one of his Bible Studies. He taught these Sunday sessions for years, well into his nineties. Numerous of his books are spiritual in nature sharing with the reader his insights into the faith that sustained him in times of great needs. While his Presidency wasn't as successful as he would have liked for it to have been, his accomplishments during his four years still made a huge impact.

James Earl Carter, Jr. was one of three Presidents I've seen in person (Ford and Bush, 43 being the other two). First, during a campaign stop in Nashville in 1980, then in Nashville when he was 90 during a book tour. Both times were amazing experiences. And I'd be the first to tell you that I was cheering for him to reach 100. And I felt a great feeling of sadness when he passed. It was like a dear friend had passed. Rest high on the mountain, President Carter. You did well. Very well.

My thanks to those who have encouraged me in the writing of the Hail to the Chief series. To my daughter, Rebekka, for your encouragement, I continue to be grateful. Thanks to the kind folks who work for the National Park Service in Plains for extending to me a warm welcome. I look forward to returning there again soon. I also wish to acknowledge the Carter family who shared their father, grandfather with the nation for a great number of years.

If I can be but half the man Jimmy Carter proved to be, I'd be thankful.

Notes